# the
# greatest christmas
## ever

*A Treasury of Inspirational Ideas and Insights*
*for an Unforgettable Christmas*

RACINE, WI

*The Greatest Christmas Ever*
ISBN 978-1-970103-32-8 - *Paperback*
ISBN 978-1-970103-33-5 - *Hardcover*
ISBN 978-1-970103-56-4 - *Ebook*
Copyright © 2022 by Honor Books
Racine, WI

Cover Design by Faille Schmitz

Unless otherwise indicated, all Scripture quotations are taken
from the *King James Version* of the Bible.

# Introduction

Finally! A great stocking stuffer that's sure to become a memorable family tradition in itself. *The Greatest Christmas Ever* sparkles! It crackles! It rings forth with the familiar voice of home!

What do *you* enjoy at Christmas time? Carols? Poems? Humor? Inspiration? Tasty recipes? Fun and creative gift ideas? It's all here!

Tuck this book of joy in among the gifts you give this holiday season. Share it with friends and loved ones as a holiday remembrance of years gone by. Share its Christmas spirit with all those wearied by the bustle of the busy holiday season. Watch the smiles burst onto the faces of young and old alike!

Don't forget to take this classic keepsake volume home to add to your own personal Christmas keepsakes, so you too, can partake of *The Greatest Christmas Ever* for years and years to come.

# The Heavenly Stranger

*No warm, downy pillow His sweet head pressed;*
*No soft garments His fair form dressed;*
*He lay in a manger, this Heavenly Stranger,*
*The precious Lord Jesus, the wonderful Child.*

*UNKNOWN*

# The Most Important Things You can Give on Christmas

*-YOUR TIME-*
*Volunteer to help those less fortunate.*

*-YOUR LOVE-*
*It's the thought that counts.*

*-YOUR LIFE-*
*Jesus was born that you might be saved.*

*-YOUR LORD-*
*Share Jesus with your friends and family.*

*When Christmas fights shine forth upon*
*The glistening, new-blown snow,*
*While gifts hang low upon the tree*
*And shed love's golden glow,*
*When Christmas carols sound afar*
*Throughout the holy night,*
*God grant you sweet assurance that*
*His ways are always right!*

*LEROY VICTOR CLEVELAND*

*Used by permission of Sword of the Lord Publishers*
*An Imprint of Sword of the Lord Publishers*

# Good Question

A youngster received a red wagon for Christmas and for days he went nowhere without it. But one afternoon he was happily rolling it along the front sidewalk when his father called, "Take that wagon in back and play with it. Remember it's Sunday."

The boy started to obey, then turned around and with a puzzled look asked, "Isn't it Sunday in the backyard, too?"

*AGNES KAMINSKY*

*Used by permission of Sword of the Lord Publishers*
*An Imprint of Sword of the Lord Publishers*

# Christmas Tree Decorating Theme

## OLD FASHIONED

*-Multi-colored lights-*

*-Family ornaments handmade and collected throughout the years-*

*-Sprinkles of silver tinsel-*

*-Highlights of red and white candy canes-*

*-A light puff of snow over the branches-*

*-An angel on top-*

# The Peace

He brought peace on earth and wants to
bring it also into your soul — that peace
which the world cannot give. He is the One
who would save His people from their
sins.

*CORRIE TEN BOOM*

*Christmas Joys: A Treasury of Old Favorites and New Gems of Christmas Lo:*
*Legend, and Inspiration by Joan Winmill Brown*
*New York: Doubleday & Company, 1982*

# No Glass Between

The story is told of a little boy whose family was very poor. He received no gifts at Christmastime, but he spent what time he could looking in the store windows at the pretty things other little boys could have, but he couldn't.

One day he was run over by a car and taken to a hospital. One of the nurses bought him a toy, a troop of soldiers. As he touched them, what do you think he said? "There isn't any glass between!"

Some day we shall see Christ face to face, with no "glass" in between.

*UNKNOWN*

*Used by permission of Sword of the Lord Publishers*
*An Imprint of Sword of the Lord Publishers*

# Things in General Never to Give for Christmas

-FRUITCAKES-
*Remember the golden rule.*

-NECKTIES-
*Silk is okay.*

-CLOTHES-
*Size and personal taste vary too much.*

-TOWELS AND WASH CLOTHS-
*They rarely match the decor.*

-LOUD OR MESSY TOYS-
*Tambourines and paint, for instance.*

*Reflect upon your present blessings, of which every man has plenty; not on your past misfortunes, of which all men have some.*

*CHARLES DICKENS*

*Christmas Joys: A Treasury of Old Favorites and New Gems of Christmas Lo:*
*Legend, and Inspiration by Joan Winmill Brown*
*New York: Doubleday & Company, 1982*

# Things to Do When Company Drops In

*-Invite them in with a Christmas smile-*

*-For atmosphere, put on a favorite instrumental Christmas tape-*

*-Then light a fire in the wood-burning fireplace, if you have one-*

*-Offer a variety of treats on a festive holiday platter-*

*-Sit by the fire for friendly conversation, and relax-*

# CHRISTMAS CHOCOLATE CHEWIES

*1 package devil's food cake mix, 18.25 oz*
*1 small package semi-sweet chocolate chips*
*1/2 cup vegetable shortening*
*1 large eggs, lightly beaten*
*1 tablespoon water*
*1/2 cup sifted powdered sugar*
*Candy sprinkles*

Combine first 5 ingredients in a large bowl, stirring until smooth. Shape dough into 1-inch balls, and roll in powdered sugar. Place 2 inches apart on lightly greased cookie sheets.

Bake at 375° for 10 minutes. Remove from oven. Sprinkle with candy sprinkles. Cool 10 minutes on cookie sheets. Remove to wire racks to cool completely.

*Used by permission of Oxmoor House/Southern Progress
An Imprint of Oxmoor House Publishing*

# MOCK CHAMPAGNE HOLIDAY PUNCH

*2 bottles non-alcoholic sparkling white grape juice, chilled, 25.4 oz. ea.*

*2 bottles ginger ale, chilled, 2-liters ea.*

*1 bottle white grape juice, chilled, 32 oz.*

*1 can frozen lemonade concentrate, thawed and undiluted, 6 oz.*

*1 small jar maraschino cherries*

*Ice ring (optional)*

Combine all ingredients in a large punch bowl.
Add an ice ring, if desired.

# "Forgive Us Our Christmases"

The story has been published of a little girl caught in the pre-Christmas swirl of activity, all of which seemed to be coming to a head on Christmas Eve.

Dad, loaded down with bundles, seemed to have an even greater number of worries. Mom, under the pressure of getting ready for the great occasion, had yielded to tears several times during the day.

The little girl herself, trying to help, found that she was always under-foot, and sometimes adult kindness to her wore thin.

Finally, near tears herself, she was hustled off to bed.

There kneeling to pray the Lord's Prayer before finally tumbling in, her mind and tongue betrayed her and she prayed, "Forgive us our Christmases as we forgive those who Christmas against us."

Perhaps the little girl's prayer was not such a great mistake.

Too often we leave out the Christ of Christmas. Too often He is crowded out of our busy lives. Remember, the best gift won't be found in a box but in a person.

*UNKNOWN*

*Used by permission of Sword of the Lord Publishers*
*An Imprint of Sword of the Lord Publishers*

# Making Christmas Bright for Family Members Far Away

*-In November, create a "Care Package." Send it by the first weekend in December-*

*-Include a dated ornament for each person, uniquely fitted to each individual's interests-*

*-Include a holiday newsletter personalized with hand-written notes from each of your family members to theirs-*

*-Send a video of your family singing or sharing current family events-*

*-Include candies or cookies which your family made together with their family in mind-*

# The Prophecy

*For unto us a child is born, unto us a son is given: and the government shall be upon his shoulder: and his name shall be called Wonderful, Counsellor, The mighty God, The everlasting Father, The Prince of Peace. Of the increase of his government and peace there shall be no end, upon the throne of David, and upon his kingdom, to order it, and to establish it with judgment and with justice from henceforth even for ever. . . .*

ISAIAH 9:6-7

The very purpose of Christ's coming into the world was that He might offer up His life as a sacrifice for the sins of men. He came to die. This is the heart of Christmas.

*REV. BILLY GRAHAM*

*Christmas Joys: A Treasury of Old Favorites and New Gems of Christmas Lo: Legend, and Inspiration by Joan Winmill Brown New York: Doubleday & Company, 1982*

The greatest and most momentous fact
which the history of the world records is
the fact of [Christ's] birth.

*CHARLES H. SPURGEON*

*Christmas Joys: A Treasury of Old Favorites and New Gems of
Christmas Lo: Legend, and Inspiration by Joan Winmill Brown
New York: Doubleday & Company, 1982*

# Keeping Jesus the Focus of the Season

*-Once a day during December, thank God for His Son and His gift of eternal life-*

*-Incorporate the simplicity and peace of the true Christmas Spirit into your holiday-*

*-Begin one new tradition this year which incorporates the true meaning of Christmas-*

*-Make a birthday cake out of breakfast breads. Serve it Christmas morning while everyone sings Happy Birthday to Jesus-*

*-Take turns with your family members reading the Christmas story from the second chapter of Luke before opening gifts-*

# Making Christmas Fun and Memorable for a Shut-In

*-Spend time in conversation together. Ask about Christmases gone by. Let your friend do the talking-*

*-Take a miniature decorated Christmas tree to brighten the home-*

*-Offer to help your friend with shopping, wrapping, and delivering gifts-*

*-Offer to make your friend's favorite Christmas cookies-*

*-Invite your friend to your home for a Christmas brunch or dinner. If home- bound, take your friend a warm Christmas dinner on a bright holiday plate with a small poinsettia to brighten the day-*

*And in the Christ-Child we behold*
*The Lord of Life and Love.*

UNKNOWN

*Were earth a thousand times as fair,*
*Beset with gold and jewels rare,*
*She yet were far too poor to be*
*A narrow cradle, Lord, for Thee.*

*MARTIN LUTHER*

*Were Earth A Thousand Times As Fair*
*Martin Luther*

It is good to be children sometimes, and never better than at Christmas, when its mighty Founder was a child Himself.

*CHARLES DICKENS*

*Children at Christmas*
*Charles Dickens*

# Fun Things Never to Give Someone Else's Kids

*-A live puppy . . . or kitten . . . or fish-*

*-A game with more than five pieces or pieces smaller than a nickel-*

*-A chemistry set-*

*-An incense burner with incense-*

*-Tickets to a rock concert-*

*-A horn . . . or symbols . . . or drums-*

There must be some deep psychological reason why we turn so instinctively toward home at this special time . . . A place where every day with be Christmas, with everybody there together. At home.

*MARJORIE HOLMES*

*"Christmas at Home"*
*Marjorie Holmes*

# Christmas Tree Decorating Theme

*VICTORIAN*

-White, green, and blue lights-

-Victorian doll house furniture painted and hung on the tree-

-Victorian dolls with fancy dresses set on the branches. White, green or blue bows-

-White flocking or heavy white snow over the branches-

-Large white ribbon draped about the tree for garland-

-Large Victorian doll on top-

# Boring Gifts Never to Give Your Boss for Christmas

*-A desk calendar-*

*-A day timer-*

*-A tie-*

*-White handkerchiefs-*

*-A Christmas T-shirt-*

# ROAST TURKEY WITH STUFFING

*10 to 12-lb. turkey*

*Salt and pepper*

*Unsalted shortening*

*Paprika*

Preheat oven to 300° F. Wash the turkey inside and out, and pat dry with a cloth. Rub the inside with salt, and fill the body cavity with the stuffing. Secure with skewers. Place the bird, breast side up, in a roasting pan. Brush the breast, legs, and wings with the shortening.

Roast the turkey, uncovered, in the oven until tender, allowing 25 minutes to the pound. Baste frequently with pan drippings.

When the turkey is half cooked, season to taste with salt, pepper, and paprika.

*PRESIDENT AND MRS. WOODROW WILSON*

*Christmas Joys: A Treasury of Old Favorites and New Gems of Christmas Lo:*
*Legend, and Inspiration by Joan Winmill Brown*
*New York: Doubleday & Company, 1982*

# TENNESSEE HAM

*1 ham*

*1 cup dark molasses*

*Cloves*

*1.5 cups brown sugar*

*Cracker crumbs*

*Fruit preserves*

Completely cover the ham in cold water and soak overnight. Take out and remove any hard surface. Put in suitably sized pot with fresh water, skin side down; add molasses. Cook slowly (225° F.), allowing 25 minutes to the pound.

Allow to cool in the liquid. Remove skin carefully. Score ham; stick a clove in each square. Sprinkle with paste made of brown sugar, meal or cracker crumbs, and sufficient liquid to make the paste. Bake slowly in moderate oven (320° F.) for 1 hour, until evenly browned.

Decorate platter with thin slices cut from the roast ham, rolled into cornucopias and filled with fruit preserves.

*PRESIDENT AND MRS. JAMES K. POLK*

*Christmas Joys: A Treasury of Old Favorites and New Gems of Christmas Lo:
Legend, and Inspiration by Joan Winmill Brown
New York: Doubleday & Company, 1982*

# MASHED POTATOES

*3 large Idaho potatoes*

*2 oz. butter*

*Salt to taste*

*2 eggs*

*1/4 tsp pepper*

*Pastry bag*

Peel the potatoes and cut in half. Put in a pan and cover with cold water. Add 1 tbsp salt, bring to a boil. Let the potatoes simmer until they are soft. Drain and return to pan to dry a little. Mash them until smooth, adding butter and 1 egg. Season to taste with salt and pepper.

Fill pastry bag with the potato mixture. Use rose tube. Pipe large rosettes on buttered baking dish, sprinkle with beaten egg.

Lightly brown under the broiler, watching carefully so that potatoes do not get too brown.

*PRESIDENT JAMES BUCHANAN*

*Christmas Joys: A Treasury of Old Favorites and New Gems of Christmas Lo:*
*Legend, and Inspiration by Joan Winmill Brown*
*New York: Doubleday & Company, 1982*

# Jam Session

One Sunday evening, I overheard my five-year-old, Julie, practicing "Hark the Herald Angels Sing," a song she'd been rehearsing that morning in church for next week's Christmas program.

It was all I could do to suppress my laughter when, in place of "which angelic hosts proclaim," Julie sang, "with the jelly toast proclaim."

*MARILYN CLARK, CINCINNATI, OH*

*"Heart to Heart"*
*Everyday Glimpses of Humor and Hope"-*
*Today's Christian (Nov/Dec 1994)*

# Christmas Tree Decorating Theme

## *ORIENTAL*

*-Red lights-*

*-Small colorful umbrellas and fans-*

*-Various types of birds, large and small, on the branches-*

*-Fortune cookies tied with red ribbon for ornaments-*

*-Multicolored sashes draping the tree for garland-*

*-Red berries-*

*-A large bright bird on top-*

# This Too I Shall Give

*This is Christmas — the real meaning of it.*
*God loving, searching; giving Himself — to us.*
*Man needing; receiving, giving Himself — to God.*
*Redemption's glorious exchange of gifts!*
*Without which we cannot live;*
*Without which we cannot give to those we love*
*anything of lasting value.*
*This is the meaning of Christmas — the wonder and the*
*glory of it.*

*RUTH BELL GRAHAM*

*Christmas Joys: A Treasury of Old Favorites and New Gems of Christmas Lo:*
*Legend, and Inspiration by Joan Winmill Brown*
*New York: Doubleday & Company, 1982*

. . . Interpersonal relationships are the most valued and cherished gifts of all. The Bible teaches that God gave a Person as a gift to every one of us, and that Person is Jesus Christ.

*REV. BILLY GRAHAM*

*Christmas Joys: A Treasury of Old Favorites and New Gems of Christmas Lo: Legend, and Inspiration by Joan Winmill Brown New York: Doubleday & Company, 1982*

# Things Never To Give Your Wife for Christmas

*-A frying pan, blender, or vacuum-*

*-A scale — either for weighing food or her body-*

*-Perfume you say you liked when you smelled it on another woman-*

*-A copy of the favorite recipe your mother always made you-*

*-House shoes like your mother wears-*

*-A nightgown one size too small, cut to fit Twiggy, made of polyester, with sleeves that are so tight at the wrists they could pass for tourniquets-*

# Things Never to Give Your Husband for Christmas

*-Tickets for two to the opera-*

*-Stationery-*

*-Cologne you say you liked when you smelled it on another man-*

*-Your favorite CD by Barbra Streisand-*

*-A book on managing personal finances-*

*-A red flannel night shirt-*

# Things Your Wife Would Love To Receive for Christmas

*-Her favorite perfume, bath oil, and bath powder-*

*-A gift certificate to her favorite store-*

*-A trip for two to a mountainside bed and breakfast inn-*

*-A candlelit dinner for two "on the town"-*

*-A housekeeper twice a month for the next year-*

# Things Your Husband Would Love To Receive for Christmas

*-An electric weed trimmer-*

*-A gas grill-*

*-His favorite cologne-*

*-A candlelit home-made steak dinner for two-*

*-Fur-lined leather gloves-*

*I saw a stable, low and very bare,*
*A little child in a manger.*
*The oxen knew Him, had Him in their care,*
*To men He was a stranger.*
*The safety of the world was lying there,*
*And the world's danger.*

MARY ELIZABETH COLERIDGE

*"I Saw a Stable"*
*Mary Elizabeth Coleridge*
*The Oxford Book of Christmas Poems edited by Harrison, Michael & Christop:*
*Clark London: Oxford University Press, 1983.*

# Christmas Tree Decorating Theme

## *WINTER*

*-Flocked tree-*

*-White lights-*

*-Red ornaments and birds-*

*-Red bows and berries-*

*-Red beads in strings for garland-*

*-Red poinsettias-*

*-Pine cones-*

*What can I give Him,*
*Poor as I am?*
*If I were a shepherd,*
*I would bring a lamb,*
*If I were a Wise Man*
*I would do my part, —*
*Yet what I can I give Him,*
*Give my heart.*

CHRISTINA G. ROSSETTI

*A Child's Christmas Treasury by Mark Daniel New York:*
*Dial Books for Young Readers, 1988., 59.*

Selfishness makes Christmas a burden;
love makes it a delight.

*UNKNOWN*

# PEANUT BUTTER GRANOLA COOKIES

*1/2 cup butter*

*1 egg*

*1/2 cup peanut butter*

*1/2 cup sugar*

*3/4 cup whole wheat flour*

*3/4 cup granola*

*1/2 teaspoon baking powder*

*3/4 teaspoon baking soda*

*1/4 teaspoon salt*

Preheat the oven to 375° F. Grease a cookie sheet.

In a mixing bowl, blend together the butter and egg. Add the remaining ingredients. Onto the cookie sheet, drop the dough by rounded teaspoonfuls.

Bake 10 to 12 minutes.

*STORMIE OMARTIAN*

*The only blind person at Christmas-time is*
*he who has not Christmas in his heart.*

*HELEN KELLER*

*The Great American Christmas Almanac:*
*A Complete Compendium of Facts and Traditions by Irena Chalmers*
*New York: The Penguin Group, 1988., 23.*

# Fun Ways to Enjoy the Holiday with Your Family

Attend a performance of the Nutcracker together. Dress up in holiday attire and eat out together beforehand.

Rent a video of "It's A Wonderful Life" and eat hot popcorn while snuggled up under blankets.

Set one evening aside to drive about seeing the Christmas lights. Stick a favorite Christmas tape into the player and sing carols together.

Collect friends and family on the spur of the moment to go caroling around the neighborhood together. Make hot chocolate for everyone at the end of the evening.

Set one evening aside for everyone to wrap Christmas gifts together — in separate rooms. Let everyone bring their gifts out at the same time to put under the tree.

# 7 LAYER COOKIES

*1/2 cup melted butter*

*1 cup graham cracker crumbs*

*1 cup milk chocolate chip morsels*

*1 cup butterscotch chip morsels*

*1 cup coconut flakes*

*1 cup walnuts, chopped*

*1 can condensed milk*

Preheat the oven to 325° F. Cover the bottom of a 9" x 13" pan with the melted butter. Over the butter, sprinkle the graham cracker crumbs, then layer the chocolate chips, butterscotch chips, coconut and walnuts. Pour condensed milk over all, then bake for 25 minutes. Let cool. Cut into squares. Refrigerate until firm, then serve.

*BEVERLY LAHAYE*

*More Than A Cookbook Cookbook by Janie Subers*
*Tulsa: Honor Book, 1986., 188.*

# Things Never to Give Your Teen for Christmas

*-Clothes that you picked out-*

*-Socks and underwear-*

*-A gift certificate for books-*

*-A trip with the family to an isolated cabin for the weekend-*

*-Family pictures-*

# Things Your Teen would Love to Receive for Christmas

*-A gift certificate for clothes to his/her favorite store-*

*-A genuine leather wallet-*

*-A gift certificate for CD's-*

*-A set of roller blades-*

*-A mountain bike-*

# Eight Neat Privileges to Give Your Teen for Christmas

*-Driving the favorite family car on one date-*

*-Taking a date out for steaks one special evening "on the house"-*

*-Taking a late curfew one evening, time to be agreed upon with the parents-*

*-Receiving a double allowance for one week-*

*-Receiving two free tickets to a movie upon request-*

# CHOCOLATE CHIP CAKE

*1 package yellow cake mix*

*1 package instant chocolate pudding mix*

*1/2 cup oil*

*1/2 cup water*

*4 eggs*

*1/2 pint sour cream*

*1 - 6 oz. package. chocolate chips Small amount flour*

Preheat the oven to 350° F. Butter a bundt pan. Combine first six ingredients. Flour the chips, then fold them into the cake mixture. Pour the batter into the bundt pan and bake for 30 minutes or until a toothpick inserted into the center comes out clean.

*CHERYL PREWITT SALEM*

*More Than A Cookbook Cookbook by Janie Subers
Tulsa: Honor Book, 1986., 188.*

Christmas is telling time—wondering time.
Wonder enough about it, and you'd know,
and you'd tell about it . . .

*ROY ROGERS*

*The Wonder of Christmas, Roy Rogers*
*Christmas Joys: A Treasury of Old Favorites and New Gems of*
*Christmas Lo: Legend, and Inspiration by Joan Winmill Brown*
*New York: Doubleday & Company, 1982*

If. . . we open our hearts and embrace
Him . . . not only to reap abundance and
joy and health and happy fulfillment, but
also for the cancellation of our sins — then
this is the greatest welcome we can give to
the Christ Child.

*NORMAN VINCENT PEALE*

*The Greatest Welcome*
*Norman Vincent Peale*
*The Guideposts Christmas Treasury*
*New York: Doubleday & Company, 1980*

# SAGE AND ONION STUFFING

*1 lb. potatoes, peeled and halved, if large*

*2 tbsps melted butter*

*2 medium-sized onions, peeled and finely chopped*

*2 tart apples, peeled, cored, and finely chopped*

*1 tbsp crumbled dried sage*

*1 tsp chopped fresh parsley*

*Salt and pepper*

Put the potatoes in a medium-sized saucepan, cover them with cold water, add salt, and bring to a boil. Lower the heat and simmer for 15 to 20 minutes or until just tender; drain. Dice the potatoes.

Heat the butter and cook the onions and apples for 8 minutes until they have softened. Stir in the diced potatoes and the herbs. Season to taste with salt and pepper.

Fill the stuffing into the cavity of the turkey or goose.

# Creative Ways to Personalize Your Christmas Cards

*-Tape a family picture inside-*

*-Enclose a favorite family recipe on a 3 x 5 card, with the name of the relative you associate with it-*

*-Enclose a one-page Holiday Update to share what's going on in your family-*

*-Copy and enclose a cherished family holiday poem-*

*-Inside the cover, pen your favorite Scripture focusing on Jesus-*

# HOME-MADE EGGNOG

*12 large eggs*

*1 can evaporated skim milk, 13 oz.*

*1 cup confectioner's sugar*

*Nutmeg*

Beat the eggs together in a large bowl until foamy.
Add milk and sugar. Stir. Strain mixture through
sieve and pour into jar. Close lid and chill.
Sprinkle nutmeg on top when ready to serve.

# The Nativity

*Among the oxen (like an ox I'm slow)*
*I see a glory in the stable grow*
*Which, with the ox's dullness might at length*
*Give me an ox's strength.*

*Among the asses (stubborn I as they)*
*I see my Savior where I looked for hay;*
*So may my beast-like folly learn at least*
*The patience of a beast.*

*Among the sheep (I like a sheep have strayed)*
*I watch the manger where my Lord is laid;*
*Oh that my baa-ing nature would win thence*
*Some woolly innocence!*

C.S. LEWIS

*Permission given by Harcourt Brace Jovanovich*

# A Christmas Prayer

*Loving Father, help us remember the birth of
Jesus, that we may share in the song of angels,
the gladness of the shepherds, and the worship
of the wise men. Close the door of hate and open
the door of love all over the world. Let kindness
come with every gift and good desires with
every greeting.
Deliver us from evil by the blessing which
Christ brings, and teach us to be merry with
clean hearts. May the Christmas morning make
us happy to be Thy children, and the Christmas
evening bring us to our beds with grateful
thoughts, forgiving and forgiven, for Jesus'
sake. Amen!*

## ROBERT LOUIS STEVENSON

*Christmas Joys: A Treasury of Old Favorites and New Gems of Christmas Lo:
Legend, and Inspiration by Joan Winmill Brown
New York: Doubleday & Company, 1982*

# Christmas Tree Theme

### COUNTRY

-Visit a tree farm. Pick and cut your own tree-

-String popcorn and berries for garland-

-Hang glittered pinecones and small wooden children's toys for ornaments-

-Cut out construction paper candy canes, stars and bells; glue on glitter, and hang-

-Make a pine-cone angel for the top-

-Put plenty of candles in safe candleholders on your hearth and on tables close by for lighting-

# CINNAMON CHRISTMAS TREES

*2 pkgs refrigerated cinnamon rolls with icing, 9 1/2 oz. ea.*
*6 tbsps. granola, raisins, or nuts*

Preheat oven to 375° F. Cover a 10" x 14" baking sheet with foil. Separate and arrange rolls in rows to simulate a Christmas tree. Starting at the center top of baking sheet, set rolls very closely in rows of 1-2-3-4-5.

Bake 18 to 20 minutes. Remove from oven. While rolls are hot, spread with icing and sprinkle with granola, raisins, or nuts to decorate.

*Used by permission of Ideals Children's Books,*
*an Imprint of Hambleton-Hill Publishing, Inc.*

# CINNAMON BELLS

*1 tbsp ground cinnamon*

*2 tbsps sugar*

*Several slices of hot buttered toast*

*Christmas bell cookie cutter*

Cut the bread with the Christmas bell cookie cutter. Toast with butter. Mix the spice and sugar together. Sprinkle the mixture on the hot buttered toast.

# The Legend of the Christmas Rose

Legend says that a little shepherd girl of Bethlehem followed after the shepherds who had received the angels' message and were journeying to the stable. All the shepherds took along gifts for the Christ child; but the little girl had no gift to give.

As she lagged behind the others, somewhat sad at heart, there suddenly appeared an angel in a glow of light, who scattered beautiful white roses in her path. Eagerly she gathered them in her arms and laid them at the manger as her gift to the little Lord Jesus.

*UNKNOWN*

*A Child's Christmas Treasury by Mark Daniel New York: Dial Books for Young Readers, 1988., 59.*

# Time of Enchantment

On Christmas Eve, the story says, an enchantment falls upon the earth. It is a time when the Spirit of a new-born Child whose name is Love, possesses the world. The way to Christmas lies through an ancient gate . . . It is a little gate, child-high, child-wide, and there is a password:

"Peace on earth to men of good will."

May you, this Christmas, become as a little child again and enter into His kingdom.

*ANGELO PATRI*

# CHRISTMAS CUSTARD WITH BANANA SAUCE

*2 cups skim milk*

*2 eggs*

*1/4 cup sugar*

*1/2 tsp rum extract*

*1/4 cup currant jelly*

*1 medium ripe banana*

In 2 qt. saucepan with wire whisk, combine skim milk, eggs, and sugar. Cook over low heat until mixture thickens and coats spoon well (do not boil or mixture will curdle) about 20 minutes, stirring constantly.

Stir in rum extract. Spoon custard into four 8-oz. goblets or dessert dishes. Cover and refrigerate mixture until well chilled, about 1 hour.

*To serve:* In 1-qt. saucepan over low heat, melt currant jelly. Remove saucepan from heat. Dice banana; gently stir banana into melted jelly. Spoon 1/4 of banana mixture onto each serving of chilled custard.

# Gifts for those Special Persons who have Everything

*A gift certificate that relates to an area of special interest.*

*A book that relates to an area of special interest.*

*A magazine subscription that relates to an area of special interest.*

*A gift packet of movie tickets to a local theater.*

*A gift certificate for a dinner for two to an elegant, local restaurant.*

There was a lady in the state hospital. She carried the card a friend of ours sent her in a little draw-string bag and during the entire Christmas season she would stop people and say, "Look at my Christmas card. The lady I worked for sent it to me. I'm not forgotten."

We heard later that card, the only one she received, was the beginning of her recovery.

*REAMER KLINE*

# Long Walk Part of Gift

The African boy listened carefully as the teacher
explained why it is that Christians give presents to
each other on Christmas day. "The gift is an
expression of our joy over the birth of Jesus and
our friendship for each other," she said.
When Christmas day came, the boy brought to the
teacher a sea shell of lustrous beauty. "Where did
you ever find such a beautiful shell?" the teacher
asked as she gently fingered the gift.
The youth told her that there was only one spot
where such extraordinary shells could be found.
When he named the place, a certain bay several
miles away, the teacher was left speechless.
"Why . . . why, it's gorgeous . . . wonderful, but
you shouldn't have gone all that way to get a gift
for me."
His eyes brightening, the boy answered, "Long
walk part of gift."

*GERALD HORTON BATH*

# MAPLE BREAD PUDDING

*1 tbsp butter or margarine*

*3 cups fresh bread cubes (about 6 to 8 slices)*

*1-1/4 cups maple syrup or maple-blended syrup*

*4 eggs*

*1 cup half-and-half*

*1/2 cup milk*

*2 tbsps sugar*

*1-1/2 tsp vanilla extract*

*1-1/4 tsp salt*

Preheat oven to 350° F. Grease 1-1/2-qt. casserole. In 2-quart saucepan over medium-low heat, melt butter. Stir in bread cubes; gently toss to coat well. Pour into casserole; pour 1/2 cup maple syrup over bread cubes in casserole. In medium bowl with fork, beat eggs with next 5 ingredients; pour this mixture over the bread-cube mixture. Set casserole in 9" x 9" baking pan; place pan on oven rack. Pour hot water in pan to come halfway up side of casserole.

Bake 1 hour and 15 minutes or until knife inserted in center comes out clean.

*To serve:* In small saucepan heat remaining maple syrup until hot. Invert pudding onto warm plate. Serve pudding warm with hot syrup.

# The Responsibility

Let the children have their night of fun and laughter, let the gifts of Father Christmas delight their play. Let us grown-ups share to the full in their unstinted pleasures before we turn again to the stern tasks and the formidable years that lie before us resolved that by our sacrifice and daring these same children shall not be robbed of their inheritance or denied their right to live in a free and decent world. And so, in God's mercy, a happy Christmas to you all.

*WINSTON CHURCHILL*

*Christmas Joys: A Treasury of Old Favorites and New Gems of Christmas Lo: Legend, and Inspiration by Joan Winmill Brown New York: Doubleday &. Company, 1982*

# That Ageless Magic

One recent Christmas I was visiting my parents who live in a mining community in West Virginia. Times were bad. I noticed in front of me, a young couple stopped near a lame man.

The husband, obviously a miner, and his wife were talking in half whispers. The young husband looked down at his wife. Slowly, a smile came over his face and he agreed. She pulled out an old black change purse. Then she walked slowly to the lame man and turned the purse upside down. Coins rattled noisily into the old man's cup. "I'm wishin' you a Merry Christmas," she whispered. Gratefully, the lame man reached out to shake her hand.

I watched them walk down the street. They were broke and would have to walk home. But I could tell by the bounce in their steps that it would not be a long walk. When they lightened their purse, they also lightened their hearts, and the joy that comes from giving had worked its ageless magic once again.

*LOREN YOUNG*

*Permission given by Christian Athlete Periodical*

# Ready for Christmas

*"Ready for Christmas," she said with a sigh*
*As she gave a last touch to the gifts piled high . . .*
*Then wearily sat for a moment to read*
*Till soon, very soon, she was nodding her head.*
*Then quietly spoke a voice in her dream,*
*"Ready for Christmas, what do you mean?. . ."*

*She woke with a start and a cry of despair.*
*"There's so little time and I've still to prepare.*
*Oh, Father! Forgive me, I see what You mean!*
*To be ready means more than a house swept clean.*
*Yes, more than the giving of gifts and a tree.*
*It's the heart swept clean that He wanted to see,*
*A heart that is free from bitterness and sin.*
*So be ready for Christmas — and ready for Him."*

*UNKNOWN*

# HOLIDAY PECAN CRUNCH

*2 cups all-purpose flour*

*1 cup packed light brown sugar*

*1 cup butter or margarine, softened*

*1 egg*

*1 tsp vanilla extract*

*1 package semi-sweet chocolate pieces, 6 oz.*

*1.5 cups pecans, toasted and chopped*

Preheat oven to 350° F. Into large bowl, measure first 5 ingredients. With hand, knead dough until well blended and it holds together. Pat dough evenly into 15 1/2" x 10 1/2" jelly-roll pan. Bake 25 minutes.

In small saucepan over low heat, melt chocolate, stirring frequently; set aside. Remove pan from oven; pour chocolate over baked layer; with spatula, evenly spread over; sprinkle with pecans.

Cool on wire rack. When cool, cut lengthwise into 6 strips, cut each strip crosswise into 12 pieces. Store in tightly-covered container; use up within 1 week.

*Used by permission of William-Morrow An Imprint of William-Morrow*

# Legend of the Christmas Tree

There is a legend that comes down to us from the early days of Christianity in England. One of those helping to spread Christianity among the Druids was a monk named Wilfred (later Saint Wilfred).

One day, surrounded by a group of his converts, he struck down a huge oak tree, which, in the Druid religion, was an object of worship. As it fell to the earth, the oak tree split into four pieces and from its center sprung up a young fir tree.

Wilfred turned to speak, "This little tree shall be your Holy Tree tonight. It is the wood of peace, for your houses are built of the fir. It is the sign of an endless life, for its leaves are evergreen. See how it points toward the heavens? Let this be called the tree of the Christ Child. Gather about it, not in the wilderness, but in your homes. There it will be surrounded with loving gifts and rites of kindness."

To this day, that is why the fir tree is one of our loveliest symbols of Christmas.

*UNKNOWN*

# CELEBRATION MELTAWAYS

*2 jars macadamia nuts, 7.5 oz. ea.*
*2 cups flour, all-purpose*
*1 cup butter or margarine, softened*
*1/4 cup confectioners sugar*
*1 tsp almond extract*

Preheat oven to 350° F. In blender at medium speed, blend 1 cup nuts until finely ground. Place in large bowl. Reserve remaining nuts for topping. Into bowl with ground nuts, measure remaining ingredients. Knead until blended and dough holds together. With hands, shape scant tablespoonfuls of dough into balls. Place 1 inch apart on ungreased cookie sheets; press reserved nuts into tops.

Bake 12 to 15 minutes, until lightly browned. Remove to wire racks; cool.

*Used by permission of William-Morrow An Imprint of William-Morrow*

One summer my family gave work to a wandering man.
In the fall he left us, but at Christmas a greeting card
arrived from hundreds of miles away — no personal
message, just a signature.
Then in the spring, he came to see us. "I've stopped
drinking," he said "I'm going to a permanent job."
When we thanked him for his Christmas card, he told us
that it was the only card he had sent.
"I wanted it to say 'thank you,' not for the work but for
the respect you gave me. It helped me to begin a new
life."

*REAMER KLINE*

# CHRISTMAS SPRITZ

*3 cups all-purpose flour*

*1.5 cups butter or margarine, softened*

*1 egg*

*3/4 cup sugar*

*1/4 cup orange juice powdered sugar*

Preheat oven to 375° F. Into large bowl, measure all ingredients. With mixer at low speed, beat until blended, scraping bowl with rubber spatula. Using cookie press, fitted with bar-plate tip, press dough into strips, 1 inch apart, for length of ungreased cookie sheet.

Bake 8 minutes, until light golden. Immediately cut each strip crosswise into 2 1/2 inch cookies. With metal spatula, remove to wire racks to cool. Sprinkle with powdered sugar. Repeat with remaining dough.

*Used by permission of Willian-Morrow An Imprint of William-Morrow*

# DUTCH CHRISTMAS BUTTER COOKIES

*2.5 cups all-purpose flour*

*1 cup sugar*

*1 cup butter, softened*

*1 1/2 tsp baking powder*

*1 tsp vanilla extract*

*1/2 tsp salt*

*1 egg*

*1 egg yolk*

*2 tbsps water*

*1/4 cup candied ginger, chopped*

Preheat oven to 350° F. Into large bowl, measure first 7 ingredients. With mixer at low speed, beat until blended. With hands, on waxed paper, roll into three 6 inch-long rolls. Flatten each slightly to shape into a bar. Wrap; refrigerate 2 hours or up to 1 week.

Grease cookie sheets. In cup with fork, beat yolk with water. Slice one roll of dough at a time crosswise into 1/4"-thick slices. Place, 1 inch apart, on cookie sheets. Brush each cookie with egg-yolk mixture and press chopped ginger into tops.

Bake 10 minutes, until lightly browned. With spatula, remove to wire racks to cool.

# Fun Gift Exchange Ideas

*-WHITE ELEPHANTS-*
*Something used, but useful.*

*-FAVORITE BOOK-*
*Write in the front what it has meant to you and sign it.*

*-ORNAMENTS-*
*Unique and under $5.00 each.*

*-PICTURE FRAMES-*
*Unique and under $5.00 each.*

*-COOKIES-*
*Bring 1/2 dozen of your favorite Christmas cookie and
the recipe on a 3 x 5 card for each person attending.*

*-FAVORITE CHRISTMAS DISH
RECIPE-*
*Wrap the dish, including the recipe; have the exchange
at the beginning of the gathering; then share the
prepared dishes together as a holiday buffet.*

# SCRUMPTIOUS PUMPKIN BREAD

*3 cups flour, all-purpose*

*1.5 cups sugar*

*1.5 tsp ground cinnamon*

*1 tsp baking soda*

*1 tsp salt*

*3/4 tsp ground nutmeg*

*1/2 tsp baking powder*

*3 eggs*

*1 can pumpkin, 16 oz.*

*1 cup salad oil*

*1 cup seedless golden or dark raisins*

*3/4 tsp ground cloves*

*1/2 cup chopped walnuts*

Preheat oven to 350° F. Grease two 8 1/2" x 4 1/2" loaf pans. In large bowl with fork, mix first 8 ingredients. In medium bowl with fork, beat eggs, pumpkin, and salad oil until blended; stir into flour mixture just until flour is moistened.

Stir in raisins and walnuts. Spoon evenly into loaf pans. Bake 1 hour 15 minutes or until toothpick inserted comes out clean. Cool in pans on rack 10 minutes; remove from pans; cool on rack.

*For reduced fat:* Substitute 1 cup applesauce for the oil and use an egg substitute in place of the 3 eggs.

# Sentimental Gifts for Loved Ones

*-Ornaments home-made out of old lace tablecloths-*

*-A favorite family recipe passed down through the generations-*

*-A piece of art made of the children's handprints and finger-paint-*

*-Cuttings from your favorite greenhouse plants, potted in a small vase that is wrapped in a holiday bow-*

*-This book-*

And I do come home at Christmas. We all do, or we ad should. We all come home, or ought to come home, for a short holiday — the longer, the better — from the great boarding school, where we are for ever wording at our arithmetical slates, to take, and give a rest.

*CHARLES DICKENS*

*Charles Dickens*
*Your Attitude Determines Your Attitude.*
*Success Collection Quote Books., 21.*

# FROSTED SNOWMEN

2 cups flour, all-purpose

1 cup sugar

1/2 cup shortening

1/3 cup honey

1 tsp baking soda

2 eggs

2 cups quick-cooking oats, uncooked

1/2 cup walnuts, finely chopped

2 cups confectioners sugar

1/4 tsp cream of tartar

2 egg whites

3/4 tsp salt

*decorations: chocolate, cinnamon, and silver decors, sugar crystals*

Preheat oven to 375° F. Into large bowl, measure first 7 ingredients. With mixer at low speed, beat until blended. With wooden spoon, stir in oats and walnuts. With floured hands, shape mixture into thirty-six 1-inch balls and thirty-six 3/4-inch balls. Place 1-inch balls, 2.5-inch apart, on ungreased cookie sheets; then place 3/4-inch balls 1/2-inch above 1-inch balls. Bake 10 to 12 minutes, until golden. With metal spatula, remove to wire racks to cool.

To *Prepare frosting:* In medium bowl with mixer at low speed, beat confectioners' sugar, cream of tartar, and egg whites until blended. Increase speed to high and beat 1 minute. Dip front of each into frosting to cover. Place frosted side up, on wire racks; decorate quickly. Let frosting dry, about 1 hour.

# Handmade Gift for Kids to Make and Give

## COUNTRY CHRISTMAS CANDLE

*-Select a round narrow log. Saw the log into 2-inch deep rounds-*

*-Collect small pine cones and other dried nature items-*

*-Cut a small hole the size of a candle in the center of each round-*

*-Hot-glue the dried nature items around the center hole-*

*-Stabilize a red slender candle in the center hole-*

*-Wrap a plaid ribbon around the bottom of the candle and glue felt to the bottom to protect the furniture-*

# Christmas Tree Decorating Theme

## *NORTH POLE*

*-Flocked tree-*

*-White lights-*

*-Ornaments: toys, candy canes, trains, horns, soldiers, elves, reindeer, and sleighs-*

*-Miniature cottages with chimneys-*

*-Mr. and Mrs. Santas of all shapes and sizes-*

*-Miniature gifts and packages-*

*-Red and green ribbon for garland-*

# Treats Never to Leave Santa on Christmas Eve

*-HOT SOUP-*
*It gets cold*

*-MILK-*
*It gets hot*

*-COOKIES-*
*He gets those everywhere*

*-CANDIES-*
*He needs to lose that tummy*

*-SANDWICH-*
*The bread dries out*

# Treats Santa would Love to Find on Christmas Eve

*-Aged cheeses with a variety of crackers-*

*-Smoked oysters and salmon on toast points-*

*-Boiled shrimp on ice with cocktail sauce-*

*-Mushrooms stuffed with crabmeat-*

*-Chips and fresh salsa with guacamole-*

# Gifts Your Dog and Cat Hate to Receive at Christmas

*-A bath-*

*-Perfume-*

*-A bow-*

*-A bulky coat-*

*-A formal portrait with the family-*

# Gifts your Dog Loves to Receive at Christmas

*-A fuzzy ball-*

*-A flavored, rawhide chew stick-*

*-A lightweight winter sweater-*

*-A chance to snack on leftovers-*

*-A comfy pillow to sleep on-*

# Gifts your Cat Loves to Receive at Christmas

*-Tidbits of turkey, chicken, and ham-*

*-Solitude-*

*"Do unto others as you would have them do unto you!"*

# O Little Town of Bethlehem

*O little town of Bethlehem,*
*How stiff we see thee lie!*
*Above thy deep and dreamless sleep*
*The silent stars go by;*
*Yet in thy dark streets shineth*
*The everlasting Light;*
*The hopes and fears of all the years*
*Are met in thee tonight.*

*PHILLIP BROOKS*

# Deck the Halls

*Deck the hall with boughs of holly,*
*Fa-la-la-la-la, la-la-la-la;*
*'Tis the season to be jolly,*
*Fa-la-la-la-la, la-la-la-la;*
*Don we now our gay apparel,*
*Fa-la-la-la-la, la-la-la-la.*
*Troll the ancient Yuletide carol.*
*Fa-la-la-la-la, la-la-la-la.*

*TRADITIONAL WELSH CAROL*

*The Holly and the Ivy: A Celebration of Christmas*
*by Barbara Segall*
*New York: Clarkson Potter/Publishers, 1991., 23.*

# Joy to the World

*Joy to the world! the Lord is come:*
*Let earth receive her King;*
*Let ev'ry heart prepare him room,*
*And heav'n and nature sing.*

*He rules the world with truth and grace,*
*And makes the nations prove*
*The glories of His righteousness,*
*And wonders of His love.*

*ISAAC WATTS*

*Christmas Joys: A Treasury of Old Favorites and New Gems of Christmas Lo:*
*Legend, and Inspiration by Joan Winmill Brown*
*New York: Doubleday &. Company, 1982*

# Away in a Manger

*Away in a manger, no crib for a bed,*
*The little Lord Jesus laid down His sweet head;*
*The stars in the bright sky looked down where he lay,*
*The little Lord Jesus asleep on the hay.*

*The cattle are lowing, the Baby awakes,*
*But little Lord Jesus, no crying He makes;*
*I love thee, Lord Jesus! look down from the sky,*
*And stay by my cradle till morning is nigh.*

*ATTRIBUTED TO MARTIN LUTHER*

# Jingle Bells

*Dashing through the snow*
*In a one-horse open sleigh,*
*O'er the fields we go*
*Laughing all the way.*
*Bells on bobtail ring,*
*Making spirits bright.*
*What fun it is to ride and sing*
*A sleighing song tonight!*

*CHORUS:*
*Jingle bells! Jingle bells! Jingle all the way!*
*Oh, what fun it is to ride in a one-horse open sleigh!*
*Jingle bells! Jingle bells! Jingle all the way!*
*Oh, what fun it is to ride in a one-horse open sleigh!*

*JAMES PIERPONT*

# I Heard the Bells on Christmas Day

*I heard the bells on Christmas day*
*Their old, familiar carols play,*
*And wild and sweet*
*The words repeat*
*Of peace on earth, goodwill to men.*

*I thought how, as the day had come,*
*The belfries of all Christendom*
*Had rolled along*
*Th' unbroken song*
*Of peace on earth, goodwill to men!*

*Then pealed the bells more loud and deep:*
*"God is not dead, nor doth He sleep;*
*The wrong shall fail,*
*The right prevail,*
*With peace on earth, goodwill to men!"*

*Till, ringing, singing on its way,*
*The world revolved from night to day,*
*A voice, a chime,*
*A chant sublime*
*Of peace on earth, goodwill to men!*

HENRY WADSWORTH LONGFELLOW

# Silent Night

*Silent night! holy night!*
*All is calm, all is bright*
*'Round yon Virgin Mother and Child*
*Holy Infant so tender and mild,*
*Sleep in heavenly peace,*
*Sleep in heavenly peace.*

*Silent night! holy night!*
*Shepherds quake at the sight.*
*Glories stream from heaven afar.*
*Heavenly hosts sing Alleluia!*
*Christ the Savior is born,*
*Christ the Savior is born.*

*Silent night! holy night!*
*Son of God, love's pure light*
*Radiant beams from Thy holy face,*
*With the dawn of redeeming grace,*
*Jesus, Lord, at Thy birth,*
*Jesus, Lord, at Thy birth.*

*FRANZE GRUBER & JOSEPH MOHR*

# O Come, All ye Faithful

*O come, all ye faithful, joyful and triumphant;*
*O come ye, O come ye to Bethlehem;*
*Come and behold Him, born the King of angels!*
*Refrain: O come, let us adore Him, Christ the Lord.*

*Sing, choirs of angels, sing in exultation,*
*O sing, all ye bright hosts of heav'n above!*
*Glory to God, all glory in the highest!*
*Refrain: O come, let us adore Him, Christ the Lord.*

*Yea, Lord, we greet Thee, born this happy morning,*
*Jesus, to Thee be all glory giv'n;*
*Word of the Father, now in flesh appearing!*
*Refrain: O come, let us adore Him, Christ the Lord.*

## *LATIN HYMN, ENGLISH TRANSLATION BY FREDERICK OAKLEY*

*Amazing Grace: 366 Inspiring Hymn Stories for Daily Devotions by Kenneth Osbeck Michigan: Kregel Publications, 1990., 367.*

# What Child is This?

*What Child is this, who, laid to rest,*
*on Mary's lap is sleeping?*
*Whom angels greet with anthems sweet,*
*While shepherds watch are keeping?*

*This, this is Christ, the King,*
*Whom shepherds guard and angels sing;*
*Haste, haste to bring Him laud, the Babe, the Son of*
*Mary.*

*Why lies He in such mean estate*
*where ox and ass are feeding?*
*Good Christian, fear, for sinners*
*here the silent Word is pleading.*

*So bring Him incense, gold and myrrh,*
*come, peasant king to own Him;*
*The King of kings salvation brings,*
*let loving hearts enthrone Him.*

WILLIAM C. DIX

*Amazing Grace: 366 Inspiring Hymn Stories for Daily Devotions*
*by Kenneth Osbeck Michigan: Kregel Publications, 1990., 369.*

# Angels we Have Heard on High

*Angels we have heard on high,*
*Sweetly singing o'er the plains,*
*And the mountains, in reply,*
*Echoing their joyous strains.*

*Gloria in excelsis Deo!*
*Come to Bethlehem and see*
*Him whose birth the angels sing;*
*Come, adore on bended knee*
*Christ the Lord, the new-born King.*

*Gloria in excelsis Deo!*

*TRADITIONAL FRENCH CAROL*

*Now all this was done, that it might be fulfilled which was spoken of the Lord by the prophet, saying, Behold, a virgin shad be with child, and shad bring forth a son, and they shad cad his name Emmanuel, which being interpreted is, God with us.*

MATTHEW 1:22-23

# Neat Things to Do in the Snow

## *MAKE A SNOW ANGEL*

*-Locate a big area of deep, freshly fallen snow-*

*-Stand in front of the area with your legs spread apart and your arms stretched out wide-*

*-Fall backward into the snow, keeping your body stiff-*

*-In same position, move your arms and legs back and forth together several times, as if you were doing a "jumping jack"-*

*-Carefully sit up, then stand. Step aside from your creation. Then turn to look! Behold!-*

# HOT SPICED CIDER

*1 quart apple cider*

*1 - 2 inch cinnamon stick*

*1 nutmeg, whole*

*3 to 4 cloves, whole*

*3 to 4 allspice*

*1/2 tsp orange peel, grated*

Combine all ingredients in a medium-sized saucepan. Bring to a boil. Turn heat to low and simmer 5 minutes. (Longer simmering makes a stronger flavor.)

Serve in mugs. Decorate with a cinnamon stick in each mug.

*Used by permission of Ideals Children's Books,*
*an Imprint of Hambleton-Hill Publishing, Inc.*

# CHRISTMAS CORN

*2 cans whole kernel corn, undrained, 16 oz. ea.*

*1 jar diced pimiento, drained, 4 oz.*

*1 can whole mushrooms, drained, 4 oz.*

*1.5 tsp dried parsley flakes*

Combine all ingredients in a large saucepan; cook over medium heat until thoroughly heated.

Serve with a slotted spoon.

*SOUTHERN LIVING*

*Used by permission of Oxmoor House An Imprint of Oxmoore House Publishing Gary Wright, Publicity Manager*

# GOLDEN SUGAR COOKIES

*2.5 cups flour, sifted*

*1 tsp vanilla*

*1 tsp baking soda*

*1/2 tsp lemon extract*

*1 tsp cream of tartar*

*2 cups sugar*

*1/4 tsp salt*

*3 egg yolks*

*1 cup butter, softened, unsalted*

Preheat oven to 350° F. Combine flour, soda, cream of tartar, and salt. Set aside. Cream butter, vanilla, and lemon extract until butter is soft and smooth. Gradually add sugar to creamed mixture, beating until fluffy. Add egg yolks, one at a time, beating well after each addition. Add dry ingredients, a little at a time, to the creamed mixture, beating after each addition until blended.

Form dough into 1" balls. Place about 2" apart on ungreased cookie sheet. Bake for 10 minutes or until golden brown.

*Used by permission of Ideals Children's Books,*
*an Imprint of Hambleton-Hill Publishing, Inc.*

# CHRISTMAS PUDDING

*2 cups flour*

*2 level tsp baking powder*

*1/4 tsp each ground cloves and cinnamon*

*1/2 tsp each mace and salt*

*1 cup flour*

*1/2 pound beef suet*

*1/2 pound raisins*

*12 pound currants*

*2 ounces citron, cut fine*

*1 cup sugar*

*1 grated lemon rind*

*2 eggs*

*1/2 cup milk*

Sift together, 3 times, flour, baking powder, spices and salt. Chop fine the suet, mixing it with the one cup of flour. Add the fruit, sugar, lemon rind, and the flour mixture together. Mix thoroughly, then stir in eggs beaten very lightly and mixed with the milk. Should be quite stiff.

Steam on low heat six hours in a buttered two-quart mold, in a kettle of water on a rack. Serve with hard sauce or custard.

*Christmas Joys: A Treasury of Old Favorites and New Gems of Christmas Lo: Legend, and Inspiration by Joan Winmill Brown New York: Doubleday & Company, 1982*

# Neat Things to Do in the Snow

## *MAKE SNOW ICE CREAM*

*-Scoop clean snow off the top of a snow pile and put in large mixing bowl-*

*-Add vanilla to taste-*

*-Add cream or half 'n half in small quantities to mix-*

*-Add sugar to taste-*

*-Mix well, and place in freezer until almost set and ready to eat-*

# Neat Things to Do in the Snow

## *CREATE AN OLD-FASHIONED SNOW MAN*

*-Stack three huge snowballs on top of each other-*

*-Find a hat, pipe, jacket, and tie-*

*-Use branches for the arms-*

*-Use black coal or rocks for the eyes-*

*-Use a large carrot for the nose-*

*-Drape jacket around body and through the arms-*

*-Wrap a tie around the neck-*

*-Place a hat on the head. Thump at least once for good measure. Then enjoy!-*

# GERMAN SNICKERDOODLES

*2-2/3 cups flour, all-purpose*

*1 cup butter or margarine, softened*

*2 tsp cream of tartar*

*1 tsp baking soda*

*1/2 tsp salt*

*1/2 tsp vanilla extract*

*2 eggs*

*2 tsp ground cinnamon*

*sugar*

Into large bowl, measure first 7 ingredients and 1-1/4 cups sugar. With mixer at low speed, beat until blended, occasionally scraping bowl with rubber spatula. Shape dough into a ball; wrap with plastic wrap. Refrigerate 2 hours, until easy to handle.

In small bowl, mix cinnamon with 2 tablespoons sugar. With hands, shape dough into 1 1/2" balls. Roll dough balls in cinnamon mixture to coat lightly. Place dough balls, about 2 inches apart, on ungreased large cookie sheets. With dull edge of knife, mark each cookie several times if you like.

Bake 10 to 12 minutes until lightly browned. Remove to wire racks to cool.

*And there were in the same country shepherds abiding
in the field, peeping watch over their flock by night.
And, lo, the angel of the Lord came upon them, and the
glory of the Lord shone round about them: and they
were sore afraid. And the angel said unto them, Fear
not: for, behold, I bring you good tidings of great joy,
which shall Be to all people.*

*For unto you is born this day in the city of David a
Savior, which is Christ the Lord And this shall he a
sign unto you; Ye shall find the babe wrapped in
swaddling clothes, lying in a manger. And suddenly
there was with the angel a multitude of the heavenly
host praising god, and saying, Glory to God in the
highest, and on earth peace, good will toward men.*

LUKE 2:8-14

*So remember while December*
*Brings the only Christmas Day,*
*In the year bet there be Christmas*
*In the things you do and say;*
*Wouldn't life be worth the living*
*Wouldn't dreams be coming true*
*If we kept the Christmas spirit*
*All the whole year through?*

UNKNOWN

I never realized God's birth before,
How he grew likest God in being born . . .
Such ever was love's way — to rise, it stoops.

*ROBERT BROWNING*

*Christmas Joys: A Treasury of Old Favorites and New Gems of Christmas Lo:*
*Legend, and Inspiration by Joan Winmill Brown*
*New York: Doubleday & Company, 1982*

Giving. Always, God is giving. Not just on one
day do His gifts arrive, but always . . . constantly,
day by day, hour by hour. . . He causes Christmas
to happen with the spectacle of little snow-covered
trees on mountainsides, in August and July; He
trims them with a color and a glory that makes
our hearts heap up as we behold them. He gives
unstintingly and constantly of Christmas beauty to
us all, if we have but eyes to see…

*DALE EVANS ROGERS*

*Dale Evans Rogers, Christmas Is Always,*
*Fleming Revell, a division of Baker Book House Company,*
*Grand Rapids, Michigan,*
*Copyright 1958*

In a world that seems not only to be changing, but even to be dissolving, there are some tens of millions of us who want Christmas to be the same . . .

*PETER MARSHALL*

*Peter Marshall, Let's Keep Christmas,*
*Fleming Revell, a division of Baker Book House Company,*
*Grand Rapids, Michigan, Copyright 1952*

# Hark! The Herald Angels Sing

*Hark! the herald angels sing,*
*"Glory to the new-born King;*
*Peace on earth, and mercy mild;*
*God and sinners reconciled,"*
*Joyful, all ye nations rise,*
*Join the triumph of the skies;*
*With angelic hosts proclaim,*
*"Christ is born in Bethlehem!"*
*Hark the herald angels sing,*
*"Glory to the new-born King."*

*Christ, by highest heaven adored,*
*Christ, the everlasting Lord!*
*Late in time, behold Him come,*
*Offspring of the virgin's womb.*
*Veiled in flesh the God-head see;*
*Hail th' incarnate Deity,*
*Pleased as man with men to dwell,*
*Jesus our Immanuel.*
*Hark! the herald angels sing,*
*"Glory to the new-born King."*

*Hail the heav'n-born Prince of Peace!*
*Hail the Sun of righteousness!*
*Light and life to all He brings,*
*Ris'n with healing in His wings.*
*Mild He lays His glory by,*
*Born that man no more may die,*
*Born to raise the sons of earth,*
*Born to give them second birth.*
*Hark! the herald angels sing,*
*"Glory to the new-born King!"*

CHARLES WESLEY

*A is for Animals who shared the stable.*
*B for the Babe with their manger for cradle.*
*C for Carols so blithe and so gay.*
*D for December, the twenty-fifth day.*
*E for Even when we're all so excited.*
*F for the Fun when the tree's at last lighted.*
*G is the Goose which you all know is fat.*
*H is the Holly you stick to your hat.*
*I for the Ivy that clings to the wall.*
*J is for Jesus, the cause of it all.*
*K for the Kindness begot by this feast.*
*L is the Light shining way in the east.*
*M for the Mistletoe, all green and white.*
*N for the Noels we sing Christmas night.*
*O for the Oxen, the first to adore Him.*
*P for the Presents Wise Men laid before Him.*
*Q for the Queerness that this should have been*
  *Near two-thousand years before you were seen.*
*R for the Reindeer leaping the roofs.*
*S for the Stockings that Santa Claus stuffs.*
*T for the Toys, the Tinsel, the Tree*
*U is for Us — the whole family.*
*V is for Visitors bringing us cheer.*
*W is Welcome to the happy New Year*
*X Y Z bother me! All I can say,*
  *Is this end of my Christmas lay.*
  *So now to you all, wherever you be,*
  *A merry, merry Christmas, and many may you see!*

*U N K N O W N*